For my daughters
Isabella and Julianna

In the end, every word
I have written
is a love note
for you.

INTRODUCTION

This book is an act of love, a creation birthed from years of sharing my heart with the world through words. A collection of love notes written over the years of my own pilgrimage into heartache, redemption and reclamation.

The words in this book poured from the depths of me, and each is a reflection of my truth in the moment of its writing. But life changes, so too does the meaning we make of it, and thus the stories we craft out of that meaning. They change and unfold and unfurl into the deepest of truth, and with these truths we weave a story on which nothing and everything can rest.

Our changing truths often cause us to doubt our own knowing. To hesitate in putting pen to page in case something shifts, making the story we've written one we no longer believe. Let this book be your reminder that your truth, as human and fallible as you are, is a truth you can stand on, and create from, here and now and always. Let these words serve as signposts along the path that mark the wisdom of the person you are and the person you are in the process of becoming.

My deepest hope for this book is that you catch a glimpse of yourself and your truths: past, present and future. That you find tucked inside of these lines comfort, recognition, and wild permission. That you discover a light in the dark, a space to hold your grief. An invitation to claim the raw and the messy and the spark of your own power. To own the brilliantly shifting truth of your life.

Inside these pages, and inside of your own life, seek out the truths that make your heart beat a little steadier, your skin tingle in recognition, your tears fall and your breath hit just that much deeper. And always make of them the meaning that you need the most.

Remember, the words meant for you will find you, always.

xo *Jeanette*

YOU ARE NOT TOO MUCH

Jeanette LeBlanc

01. heartache

This is for the ones who speak incantation and trust the gut wisdom and the red-hot blood that pounds in their veins. This is for those who are called relentless. Who are labeled too much. Who are called the names they have been calling women like us since the beginning of time. Witch. Enchantress. Sorceress. For those who are shunned, who are shamed, who are burned. **This is for those who have burned so many times they no longer fear the fire. This is for those who have learned to rise. This is for the ones who have survived. This is for you.**

I'M RIGHT HERE WITH YOU. In your weakest moments. When you know you shouldn't, but you beg again. When you know you shouldn't, but you pick up that drink. When you know you shouldn't, but you send the text anyway because it's the only honest thing to do—emergency flare into the dark. When that fight or that surrender is all we have to remind us we still have agency. When it seems there is nothing left to choose. Even then, there are candles lit in the dark for you. I'm playing the saddest song and it's filling this space and I've saved room for you here. There are soft pillows and warm blankets and you can lay your head here on my chest and find my breathing to lull you to a place where you can finally rest.

REST NOW, LOVE. THERE WILL BE TIME ENOUGH LATER TO DEAL WITH ALL THAT MUST BE DONE. FOR NOW, TAKE A DEEP BREATH, CLOSE YOUR EYES, AND REST.

It's true. Not everything will be okay. This is not okay. It's the deepest ache. It's a solid core of loss layered on top of loss. I know it is. Although it may not be okay—you will. I feel this deep and true and right in the marrow of my bones. You will be okay and more than okay and so much more than you could possibly know. There will be love. The kind of love that changes everything. And maybe more heartache. And so much laughter and breathless kisses and the hard fall of tears.

THERE IS SO MUCH MORE AHEAD. AND IT IS SO VERY GOOD.

IT'S TIME TO STOP RUNNING.
SIT HERE WITH ME BY THE
OCEAN AND LAY YOUR HEAD
IN MY LAP, LOVE. TELL ME
YOUR STORIES. THE ONES
THAT HAVE FORMED YOU
INTO THE GIFT THAT YOU
ARE. NOW TAKE A BREATH
AND LET IT GO. LET IT ALL
GO. LET THE SEA BREEZE
CARRY IT AWAY. LET YOUR
TEARS FALL.

*You will be held now. You will be
carried. You can stop running.
You can cease the endless
motion and constant struggle.
You are home. You can rest now.
You are safe.*
***MAYBE, JUST MAYBE, NOW
YOU CAN BE STILL.***

There are some things we want that are not ours to have. Some weeks will not provide you with what was wanted, regardless of how deep your desire runs. Do not deny yourself this simple heartache. ***All of grief demands its own expression in its own time. Suppression is only a delay of the inevitable.*** So let the sadness flatten you. Stay in bed until it lifts. Let it wind its way through you. It will anyway, so don't try to fight it. And remember, love, this is not forever.

When you wake and feel the sadness flood you, take a moment to honor your broken heart.

She is wise and powerful. She is never anything but exactly what is needed.

She will break and break and break again and still choose love. You know this. Do not pretend otherwise.

Cynicism is not for you, nor is lack of hope. What has been reborn will now refuse to die. Nurture it and let it live.

EVEN UNMET HOPE IS A BLESSING. WANT TEACHES, IF WE LET IT.

Go ahead and let your tears fall. Let them fall until your shoulders shake and a tiny salt sea swirls down your face and neck. Let them fall until you want to scream. And then scream. Do it. Scream and howl and get primal with this grief. This life: it is not as you imagined it. Full of blessings upon blessings, oh holy yes. And holding grief upon grief intermingled with the good. **THERE IS ROOM FOR BOTH. FOR HOLY GRATITUDE AND THE DEPTHS OF SADNESS THAT RUN LIKE GROUNDWATER BENEATH IT ALL. EMBRACE THE COMPLEXITY. OWN THE PARADOX. RIGHT IN THE CENTER OF THIS SPACE IS THE CORE OF ALL THAT THERE IS.** Lean into this. Curl your entire being around this and bring it home. Bring it home, love. Bring it home.

Grief fully *unleashed* is
its own wild muse.

You will not be able to light enough candles to push away the encroaching of this night. The darkness has its own heavy weight. There is a night sky obscured by impenetrable clouds. The stars are as impossible to imagine as if they did not exist. But they are there. They are always there. Shining and exploding and fragmenting into pieces too far away to see. The light travels toward us over countless miles, and even in their eventual darkness, they travel toward us still. It's still going to get dark sometimes. The cycle between darkness and light is predictable and necessary and true. We must go deep and explore the murky shadows. We must travel down and dig our fingers into the earth and discover the root of things. We must dance in the underworld.
AND WE MUST—AND WE WILL, AND WE DO—EVENTUALLY RISE AGAIN.

SO, LET IT FALL.
LET IT ALL COME DOWN.
CRUMBLE LIKE EARTHQUAKE,
LIKE FOREST BLAZE,
LIKE ARMAGEDDON TIMES.
STAND AMIDST THE RUBBLE
WITH TREMBLING LEGS
AND STARDUST SKIN.
SURVEY THE DAMAGE.
HOLD YOUR GRIEF CLOSE.
USHER IT INSIDE.
NAME IT TRUTH.
AND GO AHEAD,
LET IT TWIST YOU.

**IT HAS TO,
THERE IS NO OTHER WAY.**

Love, there will be days when there are no telephone booths to change in. Days when your personal Kryptonite has robbed you of your last bit of strength. Days when Wonder Woman panties and satin capes and scalding water don't have near enough magic to transport you back to the core of your powers. Indeed, there will be days when the most heroic act you can muster is changing the sheets on your bed. All of your energy focused on tucking and smoothing, as if meticulously formed hospital corners are the one thing that will save your life. It matters now at the close of the day, when everything in this world feels dirty and cloaked in shame, that your skin only be touched by something clean.

This is enough. This is more than enough.

I BOW TO YOUR TENDER HEART.
Your fierce ownership of self. To the battles fought in the name of health and wholeness and agency and truth. To the choices made that had to be made that nobody understands. To the judgement faced and the heavy grief cradled. To the ways you have continued, even in the face of great loss and sacred things stolen and all that has threatened your hard won peace. It is no small thing to survive this world. And it is no small thing to stand tall and to claim this life and to thrive. You have been the saving grace of your own survival, again and again and again.

IN THE END, THERE IS NOTHING MORE POWERFUL THAN EXACTLY THAT.

We are all in this together. In the sticky loss of it. In the ugly and the messy. In the wild spiral. In the inevitable path to acceptance that feels so far away from the sweetness of redemption. Because in our pain we must find each other—mirror to mirror, the grace of our shared humanity, the stunningly broken beauty of our shared grief. And you can let your grief see my grief and let our tears mingle into some kind of healing alchemy, and you'll know what I know. **WE ARE NEVER ALONE.**

LET THE FLOOR FALL OUT FROM UNDER YOU.

NOTHING BIG EVER HAPPENS, GOOD OR BAD,
UNLESS THE FLOOR FALLS OUT FIRST. LET
YOUR LONGING WIND YOU DOWN THROUGH
THAT SPIRAL. AND KNOW THAT FALLING CAN
BE THE MOST WICKEDLY AWESOME AND
TOTALLY SAFE THING YOU'VE EVER DONE.
DOWN, DOWN, DOWN—AND WHEN YOU HIT
THAT SOLID GROUND, YOU'LL KNOW.

*You might touch down softly, or you might land
with an ungraceful thud. But land you will. And
then, when you're ready, you can stretch your
shaky legs, stand up, dust yourself off, raise your
hands open, toss your head back to the heavens,
and say,*

"Here I am.
All that I am,
and all that I will be."

I see you, flawed and humble and road weary and proud and still in spite of the deep ache, somehow sure you've done all you can. I see all you feel but cannot speak. I see the way the words grow and swell, expanding your chest and pressing against the confines in your throat until they form the most unbearable pain, and the air around you so heavy with the weight of words unsaid. I see the way your chest caves in and your shoulders curl around and your arms hold your knees so tight that you circle in upon yourself. I see how in spite of this you are expanding, even though others wish you small. Despite your own efforts to keep the peace I see that you are a wild thing, barely confined within your own skin. Certainly not meant for external containment. I see you pushing against the walls, feeling for a crack or a sliver or an escape hatch. One day you're going to blast out of that safe little life you've built for yourself. The world will be ready for you, wide open and waiting, when you do.

You are here and it hurts
and the world feels
impossibly heavy.
You are shouting bargains at
the moon and there is
nobody else to hear you.
It is the darkest night you've
ever lived through.

You've lived through.
You've lived.
Do you hear me?

YOU LIVE.
YOU MAKE IT.
YOU SURVIVE.

You are enough.

In fact, you are more. You are more than the grief that brings you to your knees. More than the loss that shatters you. More than the love that left. More than the weight of what remains. More than the saving grace of your painfully beautiful past. You are more than you know. Come outside with me now, under this curtain of stars. Lift your daydream face to the moon, love. See it mirror your own dark craters back to you, brilliant and beautiful. Feel the truth of it on your translucent skin. Breathe that moonlight into every aching cell of your body. Let the moon wash you anew. And look behind you—because even in the darkest night, you still cast the shadow that proves you are here, solid and real and made of more than you think.

I can't make this easy for you. It's not going to dissolve. We can't browbeat it into submission. You will have to stay relentlessly present with all that you have left behind. **You cannot outrun your own wild soul.** But take my hand. Let me be your eyes. I can see beyond the veil of sadness and shame that has led you here, beyond the deep dark of your own hibernation. And there you are, on the other side, moving me to speechlessness with the beautiful way you choose to survive. If you hold my hand and look within the deepest reaches of your heart, you'll see it too. And we'll walk out of here. We'll start over. Together. Because I am here now. I will not leave you.

We are all built and broken by love. We are architects of unselfish desire. We are a lifesaving demolition team. We lay the foundation only to bring it crashing down around us. We kneel in the wreckage and scream the primal scream of the damned. And still, we love. We become the most breathtaking mosaic of all of our fragments, all of our love, all of the pieces of our kaleidoscope hearts. This is so damn beautiful that it demands to be held to the light.

HOLD IT TO THE LIGHT, LOVE. YOU. YOUR PRECIOUS HEART. ALL OF THE LOVES THAT YOU HOLD. THIS IS WHAT IS REAL. THIS IS WHAT IS TRUE. THIS IS ENOUGH.

Here's the truth. We love wide open.
We love people who deserve it and people who don't. We love people who have held us through our darkest nights and people who have left us for dead by the side of the road. We love those who have earned our trust and some who should never have had it in the first place. It cracks us wide open, over and over again. Sometimes it is too much. Our wounds cannot close when love keeps wrenching them open again and again. And we want it to stop. Beg it to stop. Please. Please. Please. No more. In our own moments of 3 am reckoning, we plead for something different, more contained. Something safer and easier and far, far more gentle. But love is a risk, sweet girl. It always has been. It always will be. And it is the most necessary, the most brutal, the most honest risk we ever take. Do what we will, our hearts will not be closed. They are meant to open. They are made for this. This is where reality lives. In the epicenter of the paradox. Right at the meeting point of love and loss and life and leaving and beginnings and grief and joy. In the sweet, sticky spill of that rough slice and in the invisible moments when heart is stitched together again.

In the end, you are still here. Broken and whole and still alive. Made even more tenderly beautiful in the depths of the shatter. **Finding your way back to the truth of your soul and listening to the song of your stubbornly beating heart.** *In the end, there is no greater testament to the power of love than this.*

JUST LOOK AT YOU. HEART BROKEN BUT STILL BEATING. ARMS EMPTY BUT STILL OPEN. FACE RAISED TO THE SKY AND GIVING THANKS FOR THE LIGHT, EVEN WHEN IT HURTS YOUR EYES.

MY GOD, YOU ARE BEAUTIFUL.

WE ARE IN THIS TOGETHER. None of us truly walk in isolation, even when we cannot sense the presence of another for miles upon miles. Even in the worst of our desolation. Even during our coldest 3 am breakdown. Even when we shut out the world and spin in circles until we collapse. Even then the light still gets in. Even then the heart still opens and reaches, tendrils of hope curling and bending toward slivers of light. Upward, outward, in all directions—seeking light at all cost. One way or another,

WE ALL GROW TOWARD THE LIGHT.

Blessed be this worthy sadness.
Blessed be this knowing love.
Blessed be the finding home.
Blessed be the kitchen slow dance.
Blessed be the magical sunset.
Blessed be the strong arms.
Blessed be the true north.
Blessed be the unmet hope.
Blessed be the unwavering light.
Blessed be the hard goodbye.
Blessed be this holy life.

Sometimes there is nothing to be done but let grief have its way. Even when you don't know precisely why you're grieving or why the ghosts picked just now to dial up their haunting. Even if you thought you were doing just fine and you had no idea that you were holding that much pain and that much lonely and that much empty locked up in your bones. You don't know until you do. And when you do, it's too late for it to be stopped. And so you play the sad songs and you drive down the highway at 2 am paying visits to past lives and you ask *"Why?"* and *"What have I done?"* and *"Please, just bring her home."* You scream your loneliness and your rejection and your *"It wasn't supposed to be this way!"* at the moon. And that man in the moon? He doesn't do a damn thing—just looks on with all his brilliant and steady wisdom, shining his light on all that hurts. And when you stumble into the bathroom and gaze in the mirror, you barely recognize yourself. Eyes red and swollen almost shut. Body weary and aching and empty and yet so full of the deep well of sadness. Head screaming and heavy as if you drank your weight in whiskey instead of spilling an ocean of tears. **I know this space. I have been here before. I will sit with you now.**

So, where does solidity lie when everything is taken up by the free spin of a nameless and borderless grief? How do we ground when we are groundless? The only answer: we don't. We don't, because we can't. This is what it is to be brilliantly, achingly alive. Alive in the shatter. Alive in the empty. Alive under that 3 am moon—the one that holds all the answers and yet won't answer a single question. This is what it is to belong to things we cannot possibly understand.

THIS IS WHAT IT IS TO TRUST IN THE TERRIFYING WISDOM OF OUR OWN BECOMING.

*If you are here because you have a story to tell, know that I will keep it safe. If you are here because your heart aches to know that you are not alone, **I will hold your hand on the darkest nights.** If you have loved and lost and gone to ground and brought yourself back through the will of your own wild heart, I honor you.*

SOME DAYS YOU WAKE WITH A HEAVY HEART. SO MUCH LOSS HELD. SO MANY UNKNOWNS. SO MANY MISSTEPS AND SO FUCKING MUCH FLAWED HUMANITY. AND YET THERE IS A LIGHTNESS TOO, IN SOME MOMENTS. FLEETING AND YET FILLED WITH GRACE. OR IF NOT A LIGHTNESS, THEN JUST A SURRENDER, A KIND OF SINKING IN AND LIQUID RELEASE. A KNOWING THAT THERE'S NOTHING TO DO BUT BREATHE AND DANCE AND LOVE YOUR WAY THROUGH. AND SO YOU RETURN TO THE HARDEST PRACTICE OF ALL, THAT OF BEING GENTLE WITH YOUR ONE WILD HEART.

How often we only meet ourselves in the midst of a great storm. When the wind has ripped us from the moorings of all that has been. When we are stumbling and ungraceful and foolishly unknowing. It's in the center of the worst that we come to the root of what is. To the place where things can become. To the spaces and people who can deliver us back to our memories.

IT TAKES A LONG, HARD FALL TO FIND THE SOLID GROUND THAT WILL SUPPORT OUR INEVITABLE RISE.

But **we need to remember**, when the shadows lengthen and the nights grow ever longer, that **we bring our own light into the darkness.** That even when it burns out, **a star is still a star**. And you are still you. And **your light is as true** and as necessary and as ever present as the North Star that still guides the sailors home. So do me a favor, love. Know this.

No matter how dark the night may get, your light will never burn out.

The incandescence is you.

There are some nights, some weeks, some months, where the only thing to do is to make sure that every available light is lit against the darkness.

And so if this is your night, or your week, or your month, as it has been mine, know that I've lit all the candles in the house and that the light of these candles is for you. The angels I'm calling are for all of us. And if you light your own candle and stare into the flame, and I do the same, I'm pretty sure we will see each other there, and in an instant know the truth of each other's aching hearts. And some-how, in that, we will find just a tiny bit of healing.

Wherever you are tonight and whatever ache your heart is holding, I hope you can find some light against the dark of this night. And if not, if you have searched high and low and there is none to be found, you can borrow some of mine. I have enough for us both.

You're not in this alone.
Even if it feels like it.
Even if you could swear that there is nobody to
hear you cry.
Even if you carry it all on your own.
Even if you've howled your grief at the dark side of
too many full moons to count.
Even if you are bone weary.
Even if you are in the deep ache of alone and
convinced of your unworthiness.
Even if the night is dark and deep and the air is
heavy and you're sure that you've cried enough
rivers to fill all the oceans by now.
Even if you've given up searching for the savior
that you're pretty sure isn't ever going to come.
Even if the sliver of hope that remains hurts more
than everything else combined.
Even if these few words are slim comfort in the
midst of your reality and you're reading with more
skepticism than faith.
Even then.
Be still now.
Close your eyes.
Breathe.
No matter what—it is your breath that will guide
you home.
You are not alone.

IF BREATH IS ALL YOU CAN MANAGE RIGHT NOW, THAT IS SO MUCH MORE THAN OKAY. BECAUSE IT IS THAT AIR IN YOUR LUNGS THAT IS KEEPING YOU HERE.

The air that is keeping you alive.
So stop now and breathe.
Once. Twice. Three times.
Deeper and deeper still.
All the way down to your belly.
All the way down to your toes.
All the way down to the earth beneath you.
Until your chest expands and you expand and there is even just a tiny spark of something that feels a little more alive.
Now let it go.
Release. Exhale. Surrender.
Lay down your weapons.
There is time for rest, even for warriors like you.
Release until you are empty.
Until you can feel the space inside you that has been so long filled by things that do not serve.
Until you are free.

Listen. If you're having a hard time holding it all today, come on over. We will sit on my patio and drink whiskey in mason jars and light some candles and maybe even a cigarette. And we will talk about all the things as the night grows quieter around us. We can hold the heaviness for each other, you and I. Because that's how we get through sometimes. By sharing the burdens, not by insisting on carrying the weight alone.

These hearts of ours are infinite, it's true, but even they get tired when they're asked to hold so much for so long. And our bones get weary. And our stories, all they ever want is to be heard and held by someone who knows.

Tonight we will let our voices rise on the sweet burn of the whiskey and whispering our secrets to the moon. And we're going to sink into the quiet alone we've been resisting and see what or who comes to meet us here. Maybe a friend. Maybe a story. Maybe just the whiskey and some melancholy music and a few cleansing tears.

WE ARE NOT GOING TO TRY TO HOLD IT ALL. BECAUSE THAT'S NEVER SERVED US. NOT ONCE. IT'S TIME TO LET IT GO. LET IT ALL DROP. SPILL OUT. REFUSING CONTAINMENT. CHOOSING SURRENDER.

Some nights demand this. And sometimes we are wise enough to stop fighting and listen.

If you have cried, these last few nights, the way I have cried. Tears that open you ragged and raw, so many tears that they run wild, so many tears that they cover everything. Like the rain here in the desert runs through the washes because the earth is too parched to hold it all.

If you can no longer hold it all—like I could no longer hold it all. Then go ahead. Let it out. Give yourself over to the grief. Let it bend you, the way only grief can. Knees to earth and hands to heavens. Let it be hard and let it be beautiful. Sometimes we are living and life is full and there is so much goodness and still—the hard hits, and when it hits, it takes everything we have. It does not need reason or justification. It does not fit in a container or explain itself. It just is. The way only grief can be. The totality of it is the point.

Grief half-lived is grief unfinished, and make no mistake, it will return. If you are feeling it all the way in and out and all around. If the air is heavy and even that strong silent moon has gone dark, if right now this is how it is for you, know that you can do this. You can feel it all, and you can find your way to the other side.

Let the darkness close in around you, love. Let the silence grow deep. Slow your breath until it falls into cadence with the pulse of the earth. Take the measure of your day. Did you speak truth of want and need and heart and bone? Were you witnessed in honesty? Seen and heard and known, just as you are and asked to be nothing more or less than that? Did you laugh or cry, did you feel what asked to be felt without holding back? Did you receive - even in the smallest ways, some moments of kindness, intentional touch, direct eye contact, words of connection? Did you take action that needed to be taken, or claim the rest your body required? What did you hold and what did you surrender and what remains? Are you, as the day comes to close, able to find at least a sliver of peace? There are no right answers to these questions. But if you find yourself tonight, or any night, in need of some of these things, or at the end of a day that left you emptied rather than filled, come find me under the tree and we will watch the sky turn from pink to deep blue to bruised purple to inky black. We will wonder at the stars as they appear and breathe more deeply as the air grows cooler. And we will ask each other what we need and fully listen to the response. And even in this, without any other doing, something in us will be filled. This is the power of being seen and heard. This is the power of bearing witness and holding space. **This is the power of us.**

Follow the roadmap of memory that carried you through. Trace the lines of sad and heartbreak. Navigate the healing and honor the fault lines that divide what was from what is to come. Send wishes that all was and is as it should and must and will be. Trust that it is so.

CRY AS MUCH AS YOU NEED TO.
IT'S OKAY TO BE ALL THE WAY BROKEN,
THAT'S THE ONLY WAY TO LET THE
GRIEF DO ITS HOLY WORK.
SO GO AHEAD,
CRY SO MUCH THAT THE RIVERS
FLOOD THE OCEANS
AND THE FORECASTERS ANNOUNCE
THAT THE DROUGHT IS OVER.
AND THEN BE DONE CRYING.
BE DONE.

STEADY UP, GIRL YOU ARE FAR BETTER THAN THIS.

Listen.

For real this time.

Stop trying to cram your heart into the hands of lovers with clenched fists.

Stop trying to cram your heart into the hands of lovers with open palms.

There's a safe space somewhere between holding on too tightly and letting things blow away in the breeze.

I promise you this.

Sometimes healing looks like falling apart. Sometimes falling apart is the path to what can be built.

Sometimes, we go through the darkest nights, and there is nobody but the man in the moon to hear. He always listens.

Now you listen.
There is not enough air in the room, but you are breathing. There is nobody here, but you are held. You have broken, and the world is breaking, and we will always rebuild.

DO YOU HEAR ME, LOVE?
WE WILL ALWAYS REBUILD.

**IF YOU, TONIGHT, ARE IN THE MIDST OF A DANCE WITH ONE OF THE MILLIONS OF DEATHS THAT THIS LIFE HOLDS, DO THIS.
GO BUY A PRAYER CANDLE. BURN IT FOR WHAT IS GONE. BURN IT FOR WHAT IS TO COME. KEEP IT BURNING TO LIGHT THE PASSAGE, BOTH FOR WHAT IS LEAVING AND FOR YOU, WALKING THE PATH HOME TO YOURSELF AND TO WHAT COMES NEXT.**

Endings and beginnings. Darkness and light. Devotion and transgression. And you, with stories carved into your bones. Heart pulsing true. A chest full of holy love and holy death.
Holding it all.
Lighting the way home.

The ache is a ferocious kind of alchemy, the catalyst for transformation. The unanswered call? It creates the space and the silence you need to remember how to hear your own voice. The unmet hope gifts a crystallized understanding of your holy need. The longing that still curls in stubbornly hopeful tendrils from your open wounds? These will be your roots, seeking through hard earth to find you exactly what you need to thrive. The grief that took you to the ground will help form the bedrock of your eventual rise.

THE GREATEST AND MOST TRANSFORMATIVE GRACE HAS ALWAYS BEEN DELIVERED BY THE MOST BROKEN-OPEN SPACES. **BE GRATEFUL FOR THE BROKEN AND FOR THE TEARS AND FOR THE GRACE THAT SUSTAINS.** IT IS BECAUSE OF ALL OF THIS THAT YOU ARE AS YOU ARE.

02. redemption

I know you wear your heart on your sleeve,
pieced together from soft driftwood and tattered
suitcases and old skeleton keys and the shards of pottery
you've tucked in your pockets from all the things you've
seen break along the way. I know your soul glitters with
fragments of love affairs and fiery passion and endless
nights of candlelight and whispers against bare skin. I
know you hear the echoes of long-gone trains and feel
the pulse of memory reminding you of things you've not
encountered in this lifetime. I know that sometimes
sunlight filtering through trees can bring you to your knees
in breathless gratitude. I know the path has taken you to
unexpected worlds, that you've seen beauty beyond
measure and experienced the sort of kindness that cracks
you wide open. I know it has been hard and your edges
have been made rough and sharp and then worn down,
again and again. I know you've been told that you feel too
much and you can't quite shake the fear that you'll never
be enough. I know you are tired, love. I know the ache
lodged in your bones. It has been a long road and you
yearn for rest and comfort and home. But I've also seen
you twirling barefoot in the grass by moonlight. And that
moon? She is dancing with the sun and this wild spinning
earth, coaxing the ocean to crash on the shore, over and
over again, just for you. There are stars traveling
unfathomable distances and burning to dust when they
enter our atmosphere so that you can breathe a little bit of
light into your soul when you need it the most. Then there
is you. Throwing open the doors, ushering the spirit inside
and keeping your rebel heart pulsing strong. You. Keeper
of wonder. The child of every revolution this world has
ever seen. What power you hold. What tremendous
mystery and magic live in your center. **How blessed this
world is to know the mystical, untamable brilliance
that is you.**

You have spent too long offering everything you need to everyone but yourself. Gather the energy and nurture the spark that lives within.

This is divine creatrix power. This is the birthplace of all creation. Pull in everything that you have always given to others and hold it close. Coax it to the surface. Claim it as your own. Hold it in your center until you hum with it. Until it burns. Until it begins the necessary process of distilling you down to your essence. Your core. Your one true thing. You.

Now you are ready to really begin. Every time you lose your way, just come back to the mirror. Face yourself again. See the one who gazes back at you, with all that she has and all that she's lost along the way. Learn to recognize her truth and beauty and wisdom. Greet her with kindness. Offer her love and thank her for her wisdom and service. Smile slowly. And begin again.

SOMETIMES STILLNESS TAKES FAR MORE STRENGTH THAN MOVEMENT. **THERE ARE TIMES WHEN CHOOSING TO STAY REQUIRES A LEVEL OF FIERCE TENACITY YOU WOULDN'T NEED IF YOU DECIDED TO LEAVE.** BOLDNESS DOES NOT ALWAYS DECLARE ITSELF TO THE WORLD AND DEMAND ATTENTION BUT RATHER LIVES STEADY AND SMALL IN THE SPACES WE CHOOSE TO CONTINUE INHABITING, EVEN THOUGH WE ARE CALLED ELSEWHERE.

ACCEPT THAT ALL
WILL BE
REVEALED IN
TIME. KNOW THAT
YOU ARE THE
MOST PERFECT,
MOST BEAUTIFUL,
MOST INSPIRING
PERSON I HAVE
EVER KNOWN.

YOU ARE SAFE HERE.
YOU ARE HOME NOW.
YOU CAN REST.

Growth and healing do not always require insistence and force; sometimes we must merely learn to soften and release.

I AM BEGINNING TO UNDERSTAND WHAT IT IS TO BE INFINITE.

Every time you get beaten down and emptied out, you are also spreading the fragments of your divinity into a universe that desperately needs you. Let the kindness and the raw, aching beauty of the universe shatter you over and over again. Find peace in the knowledge that your whole is composed of the sum of all of your beautifully broken pieces. Because breaking is becoming. We never lose ourselves. We don't break forever. We just find new configurations of wholeness.

And every single one is breathtaking.

Love lifts us, giddy and hopeful, to the wildest heights. Sometimes we free-fall into a gentle landing. Sometimes we get unceremoniously dumped from 30,000 feet. Sometimes love just up and leaves, and we are obliterated in its wake. We grow wary. Lose faith. Stop trusting. We embrace our cynicism, build walls around our fragile hearts. And at our most bruised and tattered, these boundaries are protective and wise and true. We need solitude and seclusion and distance and dark chocolate and dramatically scrawled journal entries and good friends and movies that make us cry. But time and space eventually grant a reprieve, and we are brought back to our hearts. Back to our truth. **And the truth is that we don't need to trust in love. Or in forever. Or even ourselves or our partners or the universe. We just need to trust in our hearts.** Our wise and foolish, brave and battered hearts. Idealistic and cynical, cracked and patched and still—in spite of it all—stubbornly pumping love through our electric souls. Our hearts lead us into love. They lead us out. And then—crazy and hopeful and free—they knock down walls and move mountains to try again. There's nothing to do but give thanks for the wild possibility of that tender grace.

Look at me, love. Let me cup your chin and tip your face so that your eyes meet mine. Listen to me now; this is important. Your skin is a glorious road map of scars gifted by love and by devastation. Your heart is inked with the essence of unspoken words and stories yet to find life. Your breath will always remember what it was to love without translation. Your bones are the only things that know the whole truth. Freedom is the only language your heart knows how to speak.

THE STORIES THAT WILL DEFINE YOU ARE NEVER DONE BEING WRITTEN.

I know you, your darkness and your shadow and all the things for which you practice self-flagellation. I still see you as good and true and strong and powerful and exquisitely present in this world. You have not chosen the easy way. **Life has not granted you a gentle path. Not even close. But you have followed your own trail, again and again and again. You have done what you needed to do to move forward. You have placed one foot in front of the other and kept on going—even when that was the most difficult thing to do.** You have defined your space and your territory. You have said, "This is mine. You may not enter now." And you meant it. You stood by that boundary, even when it was impossibly hard. And all of this, my friend, is no small thing. The voices in your head that say otherwise? These are born not from truth but from the stories others have created for you. These stories do not have to be yours. Even if they once were, you need not accept them any longer. Give them back. Every last one.

She had a tender heart and a weary soul, it is true.

She was tired, poor girl, down to her bones. It had been a long and lonely road, and it was not over yet.

And still, despite all of this, each night when she dreamed it was of a wild tangle of forest and the place where the river crashed unending into the sea.

And she heard the song of the wild things on the air around her and she knew, somehow, that they were calling her back home.

Decline love that requires a compromise of spirit. The one that will feed your soul and fuel your fire is one that offers full agency over your heart, your body, your creativity, and your life.

REMEMBER, YOUR LOVE IS A GIFT, A TRUTH, A HOLY, SACRED THING.

Give yourself permission to feel the fullness of your emotion, good and bad and cranky and wallowing and full of self-pity sometimes. Because in doing so, you free the space in yourself to offer the same to others. Because in doing so, you send a wave of acceptance, inward and outward. Because in doing so, you open your heart to the world. And if there is one thing this world needs, it is more wide-open love.

THE SORT OF LOVE I KNOW LIVES INSIDE YOUR BEATING HEART.

Some mornings, the world is so breathtakingly beautiful you can't help but ache. Some mornings, the world is so breathtakingly painful that you can't help but ache. Some days, those aches collide, right in the center of your chest, and you live suspended in the wild mix of it all. Gratitude and awe and hard-edged grief. Softness and wonder and devastation. It is hard to hold all we are given in this life. It is hard to become a container so vast. And sometimes we cannot. Sometimes it is too much to hold. Too much to be contained. And it washes out and over, like so many rivers rushing hard for the ocean. Searching and searching and searching for the place they belong.

For home.
For freedom.
For peace.

How about we drop the promises and resolutions and expectations? How about we agree to not even have so many projections on who you are or who I am or who either of us will become? Because no doubt I'll stumble and trip a few times, guaranteed. And maybe you will, too. This many trips around the sun and I'm humble enough to know that for sure. But I always get up again. Can you remind me of that when I forget? **SO LET'S JUST SHOW UP FOR EACH OTHER, YOU AND I. LET'S SHOW UP FULL FORCE.** I'll bring my messy humanity and my paradox and my contradictions and my holy gifts and my deep-down desire to breathe more, love deeply, create fully. You bring your magic and your laser-sharp lessons and your grace and your way of moving us through, no matter what. And let's just see what we make of that.

YOU ARE ALWAYS IN CHOICE.
Choice is not a finite action but a way of being. It is fluid and expansive and conscious. In each and every moment. Even when all the doors appear to be closed and you can't identify any options or a pathway through—I promise you, you are still in choice. When all the doors are closed. Break a window. Slide under the walls. Blast them down.

DOORS ARE ONLY THE EASIEST WAY IN AND OUT. NOT THE ONLY WAY.

EVERYTHING IS ULTIMATELY MOVING US TOWARD REDEMPTION. AND STILL, EVEN IN THE TRUTH OF THIS, THERE ARE SOME THINGS THAT CANNOT BE REDEEMED.

If you ever come to a crossroads between losing someone you love and losing yourself, always choose to walk away from the love, no matter how painful it may be or how impossible it may seem.

YOUR INFINITE SPIRIT IS THE MOST PRECIOUS THING YOU WILL EVER POSSESS. GUARD IT WITH EVERYTHING YOU HAVE.

There is no right thing, you know. And no wrong thing, either. There is just the thing that you do. And so you do it.

You close your eyes and leap and you try to do it the best you can. And given how fucked-up and crazy and brilliant and lovely and impossible it all is, the best you can is no small thing.

And eventually you'll come out of it. With all the things you thought you did right and every last thing you worried you've done wrong. They'll just be done and they'll have worked their alchemy on your soul and you'll be in a different place.

Trust me. I know.

FORGIVE YOURSELF EVERYTHING.

OUT THERE SOMEWHERE THERE IS A LOVE WHO WILL NEVER DREAM OF CALLING YOU TOO MUCH. A lover who speaks, like you, in poetry and candle wax and stardust. Who runs outside on stormy nights to howl at the moon. Who collects bones and sings incantations and talks to the ancestors. And that lover, when you find him or her, will see you and know you—just as you are and just as you should be. And they will say yes. Yes, you. I will go there with you. **I HAVE BEEN WAITING FOR THIS.**

Everything
becomes
what it must
become
to serve
its own purpose.

*We never
go through
the fire
without
being changed.*

But here we are, love.

Still standing. Fierce with the reality of love and loss. Wearing the truth of our hearts on our tattered sleeves. And yes, this one very nearly took us out. And yes, there were days when the darkness was heavy and the climb out of that rabbit hole required us to mine our depths for strength we didn't even know we had. And here we are.

Broken open by hope.
Cracked wide by loss.
Full of longing and grief and the burn of that phoenix fire.
Warrior-painted with ashes, embers from the blaze still clinging to our newborn skin, leaving us forever marked with scars of rebirth.

Listen closely, love. Even the deepest silence carries its own sweet wisdom. Sometimes—at the end or the beginning or deep in the middle—those silent spaces demand a reckoning all their own, and they itch to find voice and a safe space to surface. A place, in their own quiet way, to become. Honor the wisdom of your own silence.

Know that it is true and strong and whole and good. Know that it needs no explanation or justification. Know that it is what it is and nothing more or nothing less.

Know that it is everything. Just like you.

Sometimes the battle we brace for is actually surrender. Sometimes the security we seek isn't at all what we need.

SOMETIMES IT'S THE EMBRACE OF THE UNKNOWING THAT DELIVERS US TO GRACE—HOWEVER WILD AND UNTAMED AND RAW AND REAL THAT GRACE MAY BE.

On the days when you doubt, on the days when even the moon seems to shine too bright and you long for the safety of shadows, **turn yourself to the light and let it reflect your beauty until you remember to trust in it, if even for just a moment.** And then you go out into this one wild world of ours and you do whatever you were born to do. Whatever your wild soul leads you to do. The thing that will make you move into yourself and fill up the space and breathe out the universe. Make your art. Tell the truth. Take that selfie. Step into yourself. Wear that dress. You know the one I'm talking about—the one that feels like heat and sex and swirls around your legs like the sweet seduction of freedom. Paint your lips red and your nails black. Cut off your hair. Take a lover. Leave your lover. Pile everything that matters in the car and just drive high into the mountains until the only sound you hear is your own voice mingled with the calls of the wild things.

Trust in the wisdom
of your undecided heart.
Trust in your unknowing, love.
Have faith in the space of indecision.
There is wisdom here,
just as there is when you are bold
and steady and sure.
Take your time here.
Be gentle.
Coax out your truth,
and be willing to wait
for the answer to come.
It will.
It always does.
Until then, even the indecision
has lessons to teach.

I feel the pull of the wild moon
calling me to witness
her brilliance.
The way she cycles from a shadowed sliver of
herself
to full radiance
over and over again.
Like such a thing is normal,
and expected,
and good.
Just like we become more and less of ourselves.
Just like we succumb to the shadows
and then spin to the light,
over and over again.
As if we had a choice
in the matter.
As if we didn't deserve holy reverence for
our relentless insistence on surviving that very
thing.

What more is needed
than just the one
one star, one body,
one voice in the relentless dark?
To remind us
that there is always something ready to hold our
fervent wish.
Something to close our hearts around.
Something in which to believe.
To give us hope.
A reason to be still, to wait, to trust.

YOUR REDEMPTION CAN
NEVER BE EXTERNALLY
DELIVERED. IT LIVES IN
THE MOLTEN CORE OF
OUR ANIMAL BEINGS.
IT BREATHES IN US AND
BEATS IN US AND
PULSES WITH TRUTH
AND SPIRIT AND THE
INFINITE GRACE OF OUR
TENDER HUMAN
HEARTS.

Yes, we are all selfish assholes. We are all good and decent people. **And we are redeemed, over and over and over again, just by our uncompromising insistence on living and breathing and loving in this world**. By our continued willingness to reach out our arms, meeting others exactly where they stand and making a wide-open offering of our frail and fierce hearts. This is where redemption lives. In the spaces where we come together and in the quiet moments when it all comes apart. In the wild center of this world. In the wild center of our imperfect selves. Right here, in the vastly complex and utterly priceless wonder that is this life.

TEACH ME HOW TO BE LOVED.

We all say this over and over again, in different words or with the shift and sway of our bodies or in the silent spaces where words are left behind. Teach me how to be loved. Let me show you how to love me well. School me in the workings of your heart, in the language of your bones. Let my open palm memorize the shape of your face. Tell me the stories of your scars so I can trace them with the honor of understanding. Do you see this fault line? It is where I was broken, over and over again, by the ones who came before you. Are you willing to take that in? My wide-open eyes? My truth lives there, if you look for it. I have been loved by those who didn't care to discover all that I am. Will you be the one to see me whole?

You have sacred coursing through your bloodstream. You are the howl of grief and the charity of a saint. You've got thief in your bones and courage just beneath the surface of your skin. And on the days you don't want to feel and the nights you can't sleep, when all you can remember is the moments you have failed your own divinity, know this:

In every moment of every day, you are living the path to your own redemption.

Our higher selves and our shadow beings like to nestle together and do a badass bump and grind on the dance floor. It's after hours at the club, and there's a full-on ecstatic rave going on in the center of the floor. It's all heat and sweat and pounding bass. Bodies so intertwined you can't tell where one ends and the other begins. There's the good and the bad and the sex and the shame and the want and the guilt and the freedom and the chains—all right there in the sliver of spaces where skin presses against skin. This is what it is to live with the duality of our humanity. It's sweaty and messy and hot. It's pure and good and true. It's the red-hot center of the paradox. It gets us into desperate trouble and it saves us, over and over and over again. I have been selfish and ugly and weak and bold and brave and beautiful. I have had the audacity and the grace to follow the call of my own wild spirit at the cost of the heart of another. I have been beautifully true, and I have lived a ruthless lie out of nothing but cowardice. I have walked a million wrong paths only to fall into one of my greatest truths in the middle of the weakest and darkest moments. **THIS IS WHAT IT IS TO LIVE AND TO LOVE AND TO STUMBLE THROUGH THIS LIFE, AS INHERENTLY FLAWED AS WE ARE, THE EMBODIMENT OF THE DIVINE.**

Love. it gets tangled sometimes. The purity of beginnings become a hazy twist of expectations, the intermingling of past hurts and future fears. We are the product of all that has already been, and of all that we hope will one day become. We carry with us the bone memory of the loves that we have held and all that has been lost. We don't ever come into love without the echo of our past singing its siren song.

Can we do this? Can we find in this love a gossamer thread of redemption to coax into a late-night tangle of limbs and lazy Sunday mornings? Will you follow me into the interplay of light and shadow? **Will you dance with me here, where the light and dark within me can mingle with the good and bad of you?** It is a relentless forgiveness that allows us to return here, again and again. Past the tears and the leaving and the broken spaces. Back into the hope of more, the possibility of again.

Remember, you were made for this. For the sweet vulnerability of now. For the outreach past fear and into the unknown. For the extension and unwrapping. Even for the fault lines and the bittersweet of no longer yours.

DESPITE GRIEF AND LOSS AND NEVER AGAIN, YOUR HEART IS HERE TO OPEN TO LOVE.

NONE OF US IS SOLELY THE BEST OR WORST OF OURSELVES. WE ARE ALL OUR KINDEST MOMENTS AND OUR DARKEST HOURS. WE ARE THE DEEPEST SHAME AND THE PROUDEST ACCOMPLISHMENT. SHADOWS CAN NEVER EXIST WITHOUT LIGHT.

YOU DON'T HAVE TO KNOW THE RIGHT FIRST STEP. You just have to be ready and willing to walk into the unknowing with all of your hope and all of your fear and all of your doubt and all of your bravery.

Give yourself the gift of the pause.

Let your body and soul and mind and heart find their new equilibrium. You've turned the page and the new chapter lies before you, but give yourself time and space to take an infinity of breaths before you begin to read (or write) your way into what comes next. Get out into the world before you, get deep into your wonderful human body, and allow it the gift of existing in this world.

Give yourself a chance to be lost and found and enough silence to hear the whisper when it comes. And it will come.

Call in the ghosts and call in
the wolves and call in the lover
you've always dreamed of.
Call in your peace and your fire
and your wisdom. And light
your own candle. Hold it
high—and howl and love and
carry yourself home.

You will always be your own best lover. Do not wait for anyone to write you a love song. Sing your own, loud and clear and strong. Know your heart and mind and body and desire and offer the sweetest and kindest love to yourself, first and last and always. Only by loving yourself in fullness can you move forward into loving another. So spend some time seducing yourself. Drink the good wine when you're alone. Buy the highest-thread-count sheets you can afford. Wear your most beautiful outfit when nobody will see it but you. Take yourself on dates and find pleasure in your own company. Travel alone, to places with rich food and different culture and mystery. Spoil yourself. Then, when you are ready to invite another to join you, you will know how you deserve to be treated.

Listen. Do you hear that? It is the song of your spirit. It is the howl of your wild. It is the truth of your bones, your inborn wisdom. It is the words that have been waiting to be spoken aloud. It is the fire burning in your gut. It is the lover you have not yet met but have always somehow known, calling you home.

IT IS YOUR MEMORY. IT HAS BEEN WITH YOU ALWAYS, AND IT WILL NEVER LEAVE. YOU CARRY IT NESTLED DEEP, SAFE AT THE VERY MOLTEN CORE OF YOU.

Sometimes truth is a vicious wrecking ball. But amidst the rubble lie the embers that will spark your emancipation. Your truth, spoken clear and true, is the light that will illuminate spirit and wisdom and a path that is all yours. Your voice fans the flames that will sustain you on the journey you were meant to take. Do you hear that? It's your voice. Your mother tongue. The language of your soul. The one you were born knowing but forgot how to speak. It has returned to you now. It will never leave. It comes from the deep-rooted center of you, rises unadulterated and whole. Echoes into the world and lights your way. Fierce and gentle. Strong and mighty. Pure and clear and true.

We don't, not any of us, get to this point clean. We're all dirty and ragged. Rough edges and sharp corners. Fault lines and demolition zones. We've got tear gas riot squads aiming straight for the protest lines of our weary souls. Landmines in our chests that we trip over every time we try to hide from the terrifying tremble of our own war-torn hearts. It gets messy in there. We are dirty mirror reflection. Rusty razor blade heartbeat. We cut and we bleed. Smash down barbed-wire barricades with bloody fists and hastily throw up brick walls when happiness gets too close for comfort. We stay stubbornly still in spaces that do not serve and run the hell away from the beauty that could finally save us. Goddamn, we know how to fuck up the good stuff. We are echoes of pain born from a lifetime of pushback. We radiate it out, tender and exposed, hoping against hope that someone will finally not get caught on our rough and see all the way to our gentle. That someone will come along with outstretched hands in the darkest night and say, ***"Here, love. Let go. I know your heart. I've got this."***

LOVE, BEAUTY CAN'T ALWAYS LOOK PRETTY. YOUR PERFECT IS SO OFTEN INHERENTLY FLAWED. GRIEF CAN BE A CLUMSY GHOST.

She runs headlong into all your tender parts and wails her regrets for everyone to hear. But it is your history that delivered you this road map of scars. Those healed wounds and their jagged edges are proof of your infinite ability to survive, to knit broken back to wholeness, to refuse that the end is really the end.

THE END, LOVER, IS NEVER REALLY THE END.

Own your stories, you back-alley angel. Hold tight the truth inside of your ugly. Bite your lip bloody and embrace the humble hard-knee grovel of your mercy plea. Snake charmer yourself out of your own too-tight skin and wear your heart on the outside, especially when it wants to cower in dark corners. Raise high the crucible of rejection that has built you into what you are. It is, in the end, the alchemy that transforms.

Make friends with your
teardown. Do not run from your
bar brawl for forgiveness. Sit
with the times you've fucked
up and the times you lost all
and the days your redemption
was delivered by the hand of
the last person you ever
expected to give anything but
darkness. And through it all,
know that your walled-up and
torn-down, graffiti-covered
heart is still the most beautiful
thing I have ever seen.

Do not practice denial of self or past or grief. You don't need the façade right now. Rip away the false face. Open wide the locked-door museum exhibit of your holy history. Demolish your crumbled brick walls, your dumpster daydreams, your rusted chain link fence.

Do not deny your kaleidoscope heart. Without the broken, it could never be so beautiful.

Still, you are full of radiance. Still, you turn your face to the sky and say, with shaking breath, *"I'll take more, even where it hurts."*

Still, you return and say. *"Yes, I will try this love again. I will rip down this wall and sit in the vulnerability of this space where everything is at risk."*

Still, you coax out the shadowy remains of hope and nurture them into something beautiful and alive.

Still, you say, *"Okay, universe, what is it that you want? I am here. I am open. I will trust."*

Still. Always. Again, you burn. Still. Always. Again, you rise.

My heart, she rides these waves of living and loving as gracefully and gracelessly as can be. It's both beautiful and ugly in here, but I'm guessing you already know that. You have always been able to see more than most, haven't you? And you know, because you've lived it, that you can't be this fierce without doing battle and you can't be this tender without getting torn. And if you're at all like me, and I know that you are, then you also know that **you can't be alive without being opened again and again and again. Without surrendering to the howl of your own wilderness and the relentless burn of creation.** It's true that something is rising that cannot yet be named. It's true that it's not something entirely gentle. It's true that this is a path we've both walked many times in many lives. And it's true that we were made for this. You and me? We were always made for this.

THE AUDACITY IS IN THE LIVING NOT IN THE CHOOSING.

You are fearless enough to keep breathing, in the face of loss and pain and humility and gratitude and gifts and brilliance and confusion.
This is the amazing thing.
Right or wrong can never be anything but small things in the face of your gigantic, intrepid spirit.

WE ARE AN ANCIENT SORT OF RESILIENT.

Made for the falling and the rising. Made for rose-colored glasses and finding home in one another. Made for the burning down and rebuilding from the ashes.

MADE FOR THE HOLY WONDER OF BEGINNING AGAIN.

TO LIVE THIS LIFE

To live it with wholeness and gratitude and trust. In the pain and the glory. In the mess and the grace. In the sacred and the desperation.

THIS IS THE STUFF OF WHICH REAL SUPERHEROES ARE BORN.

NO MATTER WHICH ROAD WE CHOOSE, IT WILL ALWAYS REQUIRE A PROFOUND AND AUDACIOUS LEVEL OF GUTS.

It will be a testament to our spirit and our faith, and it will push us to our edges and pull us to our center. It will be the embodiment of love and heart and soul and inspiring commitment. And it will be brave and strong and true.

BECAUSE LIVING IS COURAGEOUS. EVERY SINGLE MOMENT OF IT.

WE ARE IN THIS TOGETHER.

None of us truly walk in isolation, even when we cannot sense the presence of another for miles upon miles. Even in the worst of our desolation. Even during our coldest 3am breakdown. Even when we shut out the world and spin in circles until we collapse. Even then the light still gets in. Even then the heart still opens and reaches, tendrils of hope curling and bending toward slivers of light. Upward, outward, in all directions – seeking light at all cost.

ONE WAY OR ANOTHER, WE ALL GROW TOWARD THE LIGHT.

We are resilient like that. Our hearts are stubborn like that. Our spirits – even under the heaviest of burdens – ultimately wild and free. And eventually, when we least expect it, the light finds its way in. It always does. And then everything is illuminated. And all of our aching pieces, all the shattered bits, all the places we think we must tuck away from the world are bathed in radiance. Only then does something become clear.

THE CLOSER YOU GET TO BROKEN, THE MORE IT BEGINS TO LOOK LIKE WHOLE. LIKE BEAUTY. LIKE BREATHTAKING TRUTH.

03. reclamation

WHY ARE YOU SO DETERMINED TO KEEP YOUR WILD SILENTLY INSIDE YOU?

Let it breathe.
Give it a voice.
Let it roll out of you on
the wide-open waves.

SET IT FREE.

Be deliciously fierce with the reality of your existence. Step outside of the expectations they set for you. Be willing to experience the pain fully, every last bit. Do the same with the joy. Allow it all to integrate into the person you are on the verge of becoming. Make choices every day. Big choices. Small choices. Don't worry if they are not always the right choices. They are yours and yours alone to make. Break walls, break boundaries, break constraints—and within the broken pieces find what you need to build yourself anew. You will be different than you have ever been. There is brilliance here. Genius, even. People will notice. They will wonder what has changed. Though life may be harsh and unforgiving, you will be riding so high on the power of stepping into yourself that the air around you will buzz with energy. Once upon a time, you asked for permission. Now you no longer seek validation. You stand solid on the shakiest of ground. You throw your head back, throw your arms wide, and proclaim your heart, your soul, your truth. And when you say *"Take it or leave it,"* you'll actually mean *"Bring it on!"* Because deep down, even in the darkest moment, you know you can handle all that is to come.

Honor the ancient pattern of call and response gifted to you by your animal body, by your heart pound and blood pulse and primal burn. It is time to usher back your sacred knowing. It is reclamation time.

IT IS RECLAMATION TIME.

Take a deep breath now. Close your eyes. Get steady. Get real steady. Feel yourself rooted to the earth and rising to the heavens. Now go in and go out all at once. Become and disappear. Stretch out your hands, palms up and ready to receive. Do you feel it? Right beneath your ribs? Do you feel it pulsing, red and ready? Call it to you now, all the way home. Feel the heat and solidity. Feel the want and divinity. Feel the pull of the tides and the wild, wild moon. Hear your howl. Now open your eyes.

IT IS TIME TO BEGIN.

GRAB A MIRROR. LOOK AT YOURSELF UNTIL IT BEGINS TO FEEL UNCOMFORTABLE. UNTIL YOU WANT TO TURN YOUR HEAD. FIX YOUR GAZE ON THE WOMAN WHO LOOKS BACK. NOW LOOK PAST THE SURFACE AND SEE ALL THOSE STRONG SOULS WHO HAVE COME BEFORE YOU. ALL OF THOSE WHO HAVE LIVED THROUGH THEIR OWN PERSONAL HELLS AND JOYS. MEDITATE ON EACH ONE, THEIR STRENGTH AND WHAT THEY PASSED TO YOU.

Honor all that they have given to bring you here, all that you have given to become who you are.

This is the strength that will carry you forward.

REPEAT AFTER ME

NO MATTER WHAT,
I WILL CONTINUE TO LIVE
FROM THE CENTER
OF MY WIDE-OPEN HEART.
IT IS MANTRA. IT IS PROMISE.
IT IS PRAYER.
IT IS NOT A CHOICE AT ALL.
IT IS ALL THERE IS.
DIG DEEP.
STAND TALL.
ROOT DOWN.
OPEN. ACCEPT. SURRENDER.
DISCOVER GRACE.
IT IS FROM THIS SPACE
THAT EVERYTHING FLOWS.

SPEAK your bone truth.

DISCOVER the root of your endless compassion.

UNLEARN lessons that have kept your heart on lockdown.

EMBRACE what you need.

DISCARD what does not serve.

BLESS your tender kneecaps.
BLESS your holy longing.
BLESS your wild soul.

I am undone.
In all the best of ways.
And in all the worst of ways.
And sometimes, like today, those feel like
the exact same thing.

Like restlessness and desire and craving
for the edges of things where danger lives.
Like the surrender and acquiescence of
head on chest and breath slowing and
syncing.

Like long-clenched muscles giving over to
liquid and like the deep, deep, deep where
things quietly grow in mystery and
shadows.

Like bones.
Like hard.
Like want.
Like stillness.

Like this.
Like this.
Exactly like this.

Your body is your home on this earth.

Be kind to it. Give it the food it needs. Move your limbs and your joints with joy. Dance. Make love. Twirl in summer rainstorms. Touch this body of yours with holy wonder. Speak to it kindly, especially the spaces you're tempted to label with harsh words and harsher judgements.

This body is a gift and a temple, and it deserves your infinite kindness.

Choose kindness—except
when it comes down to saving
yourself. Then choose
whatever is necessary to
survive.

Write the truth of yourself. As you know it. Right now. In this exact moment and only this moment. Make your words sing with the hope of you, with the want of you, with the very blood and bones and guts of you. Select the lines that speak your heart. Your sex. Your sacred. Spill yourself into this paragraph as if lives depend on it. Because your lives—every last one—do.

You can do yoga and dance and write
and meditate to dubstep until the beat pounds
through your bloodstream. Get out the paint and
canvas and markers and glitter and glue and see
what comes. Hula-hoop until your hips spin with
enough energy to recreate the universe. Spray
paint the truth of your heart across your living
room wall. Go deep into the heart of the natural
world. Get hopelessly lost and then perfectly
found in the middle of the deepest forest or put
on your best boots and drive somewhere where
the streets hold no memories and walk until you
find yourself. Talk to the birds and wild beasts.
Scream at the sky. Change everything. Write and
write and write until you cry. Cry and cry and cry
until you're empty. Find a downtown club and
dance till you sweat and ache. Strip yourself
down. This is not a one time thing. Here's the
truth: Its going to be uncomfortable. You'll move
in and out of truth and peace and beauty and
breakdown. You'll want to run away from yourself.
You'll want to run toward the first thing that offers
external comfort. But hold steady. Just like you'd
want a lover to do. Nurture that inner fire.
Stay there. Right there. Bring it home.

they say you are soft?
so be soft.
you have
nothing to
prove.
nothing to gain
from a forced
toughening of
your wild soul.
be soft
because you
can
because you
are
because you
know
that it is
life that has
softened
you
that has taught
you
that hard is
for brick

and wood
and cement
not for heart
and soul
not for you
you bend
and sway
you welcome
you enclose
you buoy
you float
you adapt
and you do it
soft
watercolor edges
blending with
the earth
and sky
and sea
so be soft.
sometimes
it's the very best
way
to survive.

PART OF THE JOURNEY LIES IN KNOWING THAT OUR SOFTNESS IS **NOT A SIGN OF WEAKNESS** BUT RATHER WHERE THE VERY CORE OF OUR STRENGTH RESIDES.

All of life is not a learning but a remembering. Remembering the knowledge built into our bones, the wisdom spliced into our genes. Recognizing lovers from past lives, rediscovering truths long ago experienced, recalling lessons learned and learned and learned.

If we were born with the collective wisdom of the cosmos implanted in our being, our task is only this: to live and seek and love until we've removed barriers that unlock it all.

release your walls
now
invite the potential
of wide
open spaces
all the way in
and know that
after endings
come the beginnings
of things.
begin again, lover
always
always
begin again.

Gather close the wisdom in your bones.

Honor the fire in your belly.

Offer gratitude to the tug and the tightness and the way the chills rise across your skin when her finger trails down your arm.

Give blessing to the heat of fever and the churning of rage and the ferocity of fear.

Bow before your holy body.

Listen to its voice.

Remember the language you were born knowing.

Remember how the body knows.

Our lives often feel like burning buildings. We navigate our days trying hopelessly hard to avoid the flames. We test the doorknobs of rooms we are being invited to enter, and if they transmit heat we walk away and look for other places to find safe shelter. We have been taught that safety and security live in the opposite direction of the flames. This is often true and wise and good. There is a clear wisdom to avoiding that which may bring annihilation. Most of life is survived by doing that very thing. But there are times in life when we exert so much energy avoiding the burn that our entire existence is wrapped up in tossing buckets of water on an impending inferno. Sometimes the only truly wise thing to do is to walk straight into the fire. To welcome the burnout, to coax the threatening spark until it turns into a blaze that illuminates all the dark spaces. To walk into the fire, knowing that we will be reduced to ashes. In the process of destruction, the fire can deliver us a new, fertile ground from which to begin again. What is birthed from the ashes often rises stronger, more essential, more connected to the core of truth than what lived before. And from this space we are offered a clear view of what remains, what truly matters, what is truly needed. **So go ahead. Ignite your life. Fan the flames. Allow everything to be illuminated by the blaze. Feel the freedom in being reduced to ashes and welcome the rebirth that follows. There is a devastating beauty here, a brutal core of truth in all that remains. Spread your wings wide. Do not be afraid. You will always know how to fly.**

Know your body as *sacred*, your want as *holy*, and your shattered heart as *whole*.

I see you. I see your tender grace, your indestructible spirit, your wide-open heart. I see your fire and your fury and fierce resolve. I see your fractured desire and your unspoken want. I see your doubt and your trauma and your shame. I see the landmine of triggers and the threats from all corners and the way you still refuse to carry the gun. I see the horrible words absorbed like fists into that holy body. And I've seen those blows land, the literal ones that broke skin and broke bones and broke your heart and the figurative ones that fractured spirit and soul and faith in your own divinity. Yes, I have seen the way those blows have knocked you down, over and over and over again.

And you know what else? I've seen you get back up. I've seen you rise, and I've seen you pull yourself up to your full power and take up all the space meant for you. And I've seen you dance. Oh holy you, have I seen you dance. And I was mesmerized. Every single time.

It is time to go home.
Home to the earth that named you.
Home to the ground that flows with that
which brought you to life.
Home to the root, to the heat, to the core
of it all.
Home to yourself.

You are called to integration.
To the point of intersection.
To completion.
To the center of the paradox and the
white heat of your own knowing.
You are called to a claiming of place and
space and intention and desire.

**TRUST THAT EVEN IF YOU DON'T YET
KNOW WHO OR WHERE OR WHAT
THAT HOME IS, YOU WILL BE GUIDED
ON YOUR JOURNEY AND YOU WILL
KNOW, WITH ABSOLUTE CLARITY,
WHEN YOU ARRIVE.**

No matter how many times
you lose your way, your wild
heart remains. Waiting,
always, for you to return.
When you hear her
whisper—that small rise
within—she is calling to you.
And if you listen and answer
her call, she will help you
create a map to trace the path
back. You can dance your way
or paint your way or fuck your
way or yell or scream or sing
or pray or run or dive or write.
There are a million true paths.
All of them within your reach.

Show up. Start with what you know. It's as simple and raw and messy and hard and as impossible and as necessary as that. Because we have stories to tell. Unleash your voice. Speak your truth. Tell your story. Because after all, your story is where the revolution begins.
I see you, beneath the surface. I see your untamable wild. I see your billowing heart. I see your unshed tears and your not-yet dreams and your devotion to spirit. I see you howl at the moon and call the ocean home and ground to earth and grow taller than the trees. I see you. You are not alone. You are not invisible. **YOU ARE SEEN. YOU ARE SEEN. YOU ARE SEEN. AND MY GOD, YOU ARE BEAUTIFUL.**

BECAUSE YOU, MY DEAR,

YOU ARE THE SUN AND THE MOON AND THE STARS. YOU ARE THE FORCE THAT PULLS THE TIDES. YOU ARE THE UNRESTRAINED HOWL UNDER A WIDE-OPEN MOON. YOU ARE THE ESSENCE OF WHAT IT IS TO DANCE INTO ECSTASY. YOU ARE THE HEAT AND THE SEX AND THE SWEAT AND THE BURN AND SOFT AND THE GRACE AND THE GRIT AND THE OCEAN OF TEARS. YOU ARE ALL OF EVERYTHING. YOU ARE THE MOTHER OF US ALL AND THE DAUGHTER OF THE UNIVERSE. YOU WALK THROUGH SHADOWS AND LIGHT. YOU BURN DOWN AND RISE UP AND HOLD CAPTIVE THE PULSE OF THE WORLD. YOU MAKE THE GODS TREMBLE.

IF SOMEONE TELLS YOU
THAT YOU ARE TOO
MUCH FOR THEM, THE
ONLY TRUTH YOU NEED
TO REMEMBER IS THIS:

IT IS HIGHLY LIKELY THAT
THEY ARE NOT NOW, AND
NEVER COULD HAVE BEEN,
NEARLY ENOUGH FOR

YOU

You are complete into and of yourself. You are brokenhearted and lonely and utterly alone and surrounded by all of this world. You are missing and mourning. But you are fiercely alive and whole. **AND THIS IS YOUR LIFE TO LIVE.** Know that it is all yours, as is the whole of this life. It is yours, and it is good.

HONOR YOUR WILD. YOUR WOLF. YOUR HARD-EARNED HOWL.

Honor the life that brought you to is moment, to the unfettered and unleashed you that is finding herself more and more each day. This you knows the raw and the grit and the lonely and the bliss and the joy and the holy giving of thanks. She holds her yes and her know close, and offers them wholeheartedly.

PAY ATTENTION. SHE IS HERE TO TEACH YOU OF YOUR POWER.

Everything changes the moment you refuse to ever again apologize for the truth of yourself or your body or your wild and untamable spirit. Once you fully claim your hard-won autonomy and your absolute sovereignty of self, the real and true apologies—the ones that are necessary and deserved and must be said—begin to come more easily and more freely and from deep within.

That kind of agency, claimed and uncompromising, leaves space to be wrong and to be humble and to open wide to whatever may come.

IN ANY LIFE THERE IS A TIME TO SPEAK—CLEAR AND STRONG AND TRUE.

Hours and minutes when your voice will be the only thing that can deliver you through to what comes next. When coming clean is the grace that serves and saves. When you must unleash your truest story and stand tall and true in the aftermath.

LISTEN TO ME NOW.
I PROMISE YOU.
YOU CAN DO THIS.

Damn the consequences.

Even the worst of what you can imagine will figure itself out eventually.

And there you will be at the end—standing tall in the midst of it all.

You.

Beautiful, beautiful you.

YOU TAKE MY BREATH AWAY.

JUST LOOK AROUND YOU.
AT THE BEAUTY AND THE BLISS.
AT THE TERROR AND THE TEARDOWN.
AT THE UTTER CERTAINTY AND EVERY LAST UNKNOWN.
IT IS ALL A PART OF YOUR STORY.
PART OF HOW YOU WERE MADE.
EMBERS OF GRACE AND GRIT.
ASHES OF BREAKDOWN AND BREAKTHROUGH.
BORN OF FIRE. MADE OF LIGHT.

BADASS WITH A SIDE OF SACRED

WISDOM

EXPLODING LIKE FIREWORKS
ACROSS THE NIGHT SKY.

What are you doing right now?

Stop it. Sit down. Exhale.

Let it go. You don't need to clean the kitchen. You don't need to finish that email. You don't need to do anything but give yourself over to the moment.

HOW COULD YOU BEST LOVE YOURSELF RIGHT NOW?

WHAT COULD YOU OFFER YOUR SACRED SOUL?

Do that. Exactly that. Only that.

WHAT DO YOU NEED, LOVER? WHAT YOU DO YOU WANT?

Stop quieting that inner voice that whispers in the night. Trust in the integrity of your own knowing. Let your hope teach you. Let the longing of your holy body lead you home. Claim this as your own. Give yourself to it fully. There is nothing else more worthy in this exact moment. Everything else will wait. This time is for you. Do you need permission? I am giving it to you now. This moment. This night. This darkness. It is yours. Do with it what you will—but do it with all of you. It is what the universe demands. Your life will accept no less. I will accept no less. Go, give yourself over to the night.

You were made for the ebb and flow. Just like the ocean. Just like the cycles of the moon. Just like the movement from dark to light to dark again. You were born to shift and be selfish and howl and get messy. You were made to create beauty and to make crazy love and to find the bliss right at the center of our raw, aching parts. That's the heart of life, the center of the paradox.

To hell with balance.

You're too fierce, too elemental, too unabashedly you to be something as mild and tame as balanced.

And that's fucking hot. I'm sure the universe will agree that you, living in the fullness of your perfectly unbalanced self, is a damn good way to keep the heat turned all the way up and the love turned all the way on. No balancing act required.

So don't wait to fall off the tightrope. Take a flying leap. Trust your wings. And the unsteady ground that greets you will be perfect and exhilarating and true.

Just like you.

Millions of meteors burn, every day,
as they enter the atmosphere.
Incinerate and turn to dust.
Disintegrate into the finest particles.

Every time you breathe, you are
inhaling the universe. Right now,
this very moment, your lungs are
filled with stardust. Keep breathing
in the stars every time you sing.
Stretch in asana and exhale divinity.

Know that you are made of this
universe and this universe was
made for you. The very atoms that
have made you whole are formed
from stardust.

Your light? It's inborn. It's been in
you since the beginning before the
beginning. And it will still be here in
the end after the end.

There is no bargain to be made between wholeness and goodness. Between desire and divinity. You need not choose. They are the very same thing. They always have been. So tell me what you want. I am listening.

Life can be fucking hard. It's relentless, really. You are weary and worn down and exhausted. You wonder sometimes, will it ever ease up? And then it does. Just like that. The exact thing you had been longing for, wrapped with a bow and delivered to your doorstep. Right when you least expected it. Right when you needed it most. The sky clears. Burdens lift. Old, limiting stories are wiped out. Boom. Long-dwelled-upon fears rendered entirely obsolete. The universe smiles and says, "*Here, take this. It's for you. You've been so brave and so patient. I've been waiting for just the right time to give it to you.*" Things are possible today that were impossible yesterday. Perfection? Little chance. A free ride? Certainly not. Smooth sailing from here on out? Un-freaking-likely. But still, in that moment, when the news is delivered, the sun is shining like possibility incarnate. You're driving down the freeway with the windows down and your hair blowing crazy in the wind. The song on the stereo is your Hollywood soundtrack, perfect for the moment. Like the universe dialed in the most utterly perfect setting just for this occasion. And then that one piece of news shifts your trajectory in an utterly essential way, and you feel yourself settle into space just a little bit differently. In that moment, your eyes shine and your mouth curves into a smile. In that moment, you let out a powerful exhale and speak some divine gratitude. In that moment, it is perfectly clear. **Anything could happen. It can. And it will. And it does. And there is nothing to say but thank you.**

You can hold up entire worlds with the force of your love. You nurture and you hold and you knit together and you dry tears and you heal the wounds of this world. *And it's true—you can do it all by yourself, without even a bit of help. Don't think we don't see your strength. Don't for a second think we don't honor your ferocity and tenacity and all that blessed grit. After all, that grit is what has kept you here.*

SOMETIMES THE ONLY WAY OUT OF THE SHADOWS IS TO STEP DIRECTLY, HARD AND UNFLINCHING, INTO THE LIGHT. THAT SOFTNESS YOU PRIDE YOURSELF ON? IT WILL RETURN. IT WILL BE TIME FOR THAT AGAIN SOON. BUT NOW? NOW IS TIME FOR FIERCE RESOLVE. FOR A WILLINGNESS TO BEND INTO THE BREAK. TO BRING IT ALL THE WAY HOME. DON'T WORRY, DEAR GIRL. IF THERE IS ONE THING YOU KNOW FOR SURE AND CERTAIN, IT IS THAT

YOU WILL ALWAYS
RISE.

This story is always yours for the telling. This has always been yours. You can expand to fill it all or take up the smallest corner. You can write in invisible ink. You can tell your story in red wine stains and spilled ink and bite marks. You can only write in pencil so it can always be erased. You can write in layers and turn the page and write sideways. You can spin spirals and make your words dance. You can ink it on the surface of your skin or x-ray vision the story onto the blank canvas of your bones. You can write a novel and then let the whole thing dissolve in the waves. You can write the truth and bury it in the ground, throw it in the fire, fold it into paper airplanes and watch it fly, roll it into a note in a bottle and toss it in the ocean and let it find its own way home. Or you can share it with the whole fucking world. You can care and not care and care-not-care all at once. ***But you get to write. And you get to choose the story you tell.*** And there's no freedom bigger or bolder or braver than that.

Evolution is eternal. Don't ever be fooled that who you are now is who you will be. Be open to that which seeks to transform you. You are a work of art in continuous progress. We all are.

YOUR BECOMING IS THE MOST BEAUTIFUL THING I HAVE EVER WITNESSED.

YOUR WILD
HEART IS THE
TRUTH OF YOU.
AND YOU ARE
THE TRUTH OF
YOUR WILD
HEART.

Be gentle. **Pay attention.** Offer purposeful healing. Seek equilibrium. Unfreeze, slowly. Stretch yourself out into the world. **Let your eyes calibrate to this new light** and notice how it caresses the lines and curves and soft and hard of you. Allow your mouth to twist and stumble around new shapes. Be so very sensory. **Notice everything.** From every angle. The way your bones feel. The way you **orient to space and time.** Invite your whole being into this new way of living, into the totality and wholeness of it. **Let it be strange and uncomfortable** and painful and stiff. **Let it be magical** and novel and unfamiliar and entirely wonderful. **Follow the whispers where they lead.**

Define your own space. **Remember your own divinity.**

You have a responsibility to this existence to **live in fullness of your truth** and art and purpose. Do not be diminished by circumstance or opinion or judgement.

Your story is your own; nobody can write it but you. You hold the paper, you choose the pen, and you **write your life** the way only you can.

If someone tries to build you a box, rip that fucker apart and use the wood to build yourself a stage, then **ditch your indoor voice and sing it loud.**

A gilded cage is still confinement. People are **not meant to live quietly** in small containers, no matter how beautiful.

You are a wild child—only the open air of freedom will do.

If you feel trapped or small or lost, take the freedom to run for the sea and to heed her wild call. Hear the whisper through mountaintop pines speaking ancient truth and know deep in your bones that the forest will hold your sacred vows. Burn sage and creosote and speak ancient incantations and call forth the goddess. Splash paint on canvas under the full pink moon while the coyote howls and the fire rages. Do not fear the wild power that wells up from within on such a night. Embrace it. It has the power to save you.

YOU NEVER WERE LIKE THE REST OF THEM. THE ONES WHOSE PERIPHERAL VISION NEVER SAW PAST THE NEAREST HORIZON. THE BLOOM WHERE YOU'RE PLANTED—STAY CLOSE TO HOME, SAFETY FIRST, KEEP THE SAME FRIENDS AND THE SAME JOB AND THE SAME HABITS—FOREVER AND EVER, AMEN. NO, NOT YOU.

Your restless rose up early. Teased you every time you felt that faraway wind tangle through your hair. You were always called elsewhere. A daydreamer. A wanderer. An explorer of worlds nobody else could see. Long before you could leave, you learned the limitlessness of your own mind. No geographic boundaries or sensible borders for you.

YOU WERE MADE TO MOVE.

Your life belongs to you now. Your life and your story and your body and your precious wild heart. Every last bit of what makes you the miracle that you are. Regardless of what the rest of the world demands, here, there is no compromise. No settling. No making do. This is reclamation. This is hallowed ground. And it is entirely true. Nothing is forbidden. In the wild that is your home, nothing is ever forbidden. Not now, not ever again. Welcome to your life, wild one. Welcome all the way home.

Lay it all out. Leave your inside voice behind. Scream 'til your voice threatens to leave, and then wail some more.

Let it loose. Get primal and raw and messy. Cry all the tears you've sealed deep inside. Every secret passage scrawled in your journal and kept under lock and key. Every smothered bit of knowing you've kept locked down deep in your bones.

Let it go. There is nothing to be gained by holding on any longer.

Life calls for one thing and one thing only: that you live from the clear and present center of yourself. That you live as blazing testament to your truth, whatever that may be. Wherever it might take you. Whoever you lose or leave along the way.

Your truth sounds exactly like freedom.

DO YOU REMEMBER A TIME WHEN YOU WERE FREE?

When your heart beat steady with pulse of sun and moon and tide and you could dive under the waves and fly higher than the trees and always come back home. When you were one with dark rich earth and the green of all that is alive and the creatures that move unseen in the dark. When you knew the truth. In your bones. And you knew when it came down to it you were just like those wild things, you were kin to the storm and you rose with the sun and spun circles around the earth.

YOU WERE WILD.

IN A WORLD THAT
REQUIRES
ASSIMILATION, YOU
REMAINING YOU IS ONE
HELL OF A WILD RIDE.
IT'S THE CRAZIEST
THING. IT'S THE
RISKIEST THING. IT'S
THE MOST IMPOSSIBLE
THING. IT'S THE MOST
NECESSARY THING. IT'S
THE MOST BEAUTIFUL
THING. IT IS, IN THE
END, THE ONLY THING.

I'm not supposed to like this about myself. This selfish that lives inside. Supposed to keep it hidden. Soften it for you. Take the rough off my edges. Round out my sharp corners. I am told they are wrong. The wants. The excessive need for solitude. For life on my own terms. Not ladylike. Not generous. Not mother. That I'm not who you knew. Not who you know, even. I don't like it. But then I do. My wants speak to my needs which translate the terms of my survival. The compulsions of art that will drive me and put me at war and seduce me into the crucible at the center of pure creation. There's alchemy in owning it all. Unabashed. Unapologetic. Without shame.

I don't care anymore what I'm supposed
to say.
This is my story.
You can listen if you want.
You can join me if you will.
Because these words and this life are
my own.
Even when it contradicts itself.
Even when I make every sense and no
sense at all.
Even when it changes from minute to
minute.
Whether they ring true or untrue.

THESE THINGS ARE NOBODY'S BUT MINE. AND I'VE GOT A STORY TO TELL. AND SO I BEGIN.

Light your candles and pour yourself a drink.

Séance your ghosts and seduce your muse. Dance only for yourself. Make it hot. Feel the truth of your bones leading the way. And don't let me try to tell you a single thing about your own truth or your life or your creativity or the ways and hows and whys of your loving or your life or your words. You know how it is for you. You've always known. So quit the excuses. All you need is a blank page and a good fucking pen. Sit down. Breathe deep.

Own that burning drive inside you. And write the fuck out of your life.

Still, you are full of radiance. Still, you turn your face to the sky and say, with shaking breath, *"I'll take more, even where it hurts."*

Still, you return and say. *"Yes, I will try this love again. I will rip down this wall and sit in the vulnerability of this space where everything is at risk."*

Still, you coax out the shadowy remains of hope and nurture them into something beautiful and alive.

Still, you say, *"Okay, universe, what is it that you want? I am here. I am open. I will trust."*

Still. Always. Again, you burn. Still. Always. Again, you rise.

Show up for yourself.

Show up as yourself.

Show up on your own time. In your own way. Show up with your wild broken open heart. With your tear-stained face.

Show up with ink on your hands and paint on your clothes.

Show up terrified and full of doubt that this will never work. With all your hopes and every last thing you can no longer believe in.

Show up to announce your letting go.

Show up with whatever scraps you have left.

Show up full force, guns blazing.

Show up ready to burn that shit down.

Show up, heart red and pulsing, ready to rebuild.

Show up to break the chains, to smash the cage. To say once and for all, "I am done with restraint."

Show up to create. Open your arms. Let your voice ring clear. Tell them "Here I am. All that I am."

Tell them that you won't play small for one more day. Tell them you're here for a reason.

Tell them the resistance is over. The walls have fallen. The people are dancing in the streets.

Show up and change their minds.

Show up and change your own damn mind.

JUST SHOW UP.
EVERYTHING CHANGES WHEN YOU DO.

YOU TAKE ALL THAT TOO MUCH AND YOU CHANNEL IT. YOU GATHER EVERY LAST EMBER OF YOUR TOO-MUCH BROKEN HEART AND YOU LIGHT THAT FLAME.

In doing so, you call forth the others and you sing the song that brings us home. And then you—in your infinite, perfect too-muchness—unleash it all on the world. And you go and love too much and you cry too much and you swear too much. Fall in love too fast and get sad too often and laugh too loudly and demand with clarity the exact terms of your own desired existence.

DON'T YOU DARE CONSIDER DOING ANYTHING BUT THAT.

Look back over what has passed. Look forward to what is to come. Bless it all—not with saccharine gratitude but with the kind of raw and holy blessing that honors the blood and guts and gore and heat and sex and hard work and giving up and giving in and the howl of loss and burning down and rising again. Bless every last sacred bit—it's the stuff from which a life is built.

Your life. The only one you will ever have.

Unlock it, poet
Let loose the words
Unconstrain your endless restraint
Seduce your muse
Release your wild
Welcome this rebellion
Usher it inside
Sit it down by the fire
And dance into the night.

You are an uprising
A revolution unto yourself
The scarcity is over
The rationing has ended
and there are words enough
for all of us.

This is the root of your commitment
The space of your deepest promise
That eternal vow
To live out loud
To speak freedom
To own the deep
Of your existence
To know it is true
And good
And worthy and whole.

Tell me. What is it that you want? Right now. Don't be shy. Don't look away. I'm right here. I'm listening. There's nothing else I need right now.

You, and the truth. So what do you want? Say it. Out loud. Even if you never have before. Especially if you never have before. Tell me where your desire lives. What calls your want home to you? Show me the spaces where you are insatiable. What brings forth that low moan at the base of your throat? What touch makes ancient tremor and shiver rise along your spine? What brings you to your knees? The time has come to feel the weight and heat of it. To let it take shape and form. Feel it spiral deep inside you. Feel it gather force and radiate outwards. **Hold the power of it. Feel its mighty urgency. Welcome its holy heat.** Are you afraid to speak it? Why? Has someone told you that this is not to be spoken of? That you mustn't give it a voice? That you certainty can't ask for it? That good girls don't do that? That ends now. Right here. Not for a second longer. This is a lie that has never served to do anything but keep you small and complacent.

And you are anything but small. So shed the shame of your sex, goddess. It's not yours to hold. It never was. Your desire is here to teach you. It awaits a response. You were born to answer its call.

Come here,
Come closer.
Do you feel my breath?
Good.
Do not
look away.
Right now you are
mine.
Right now
I am
lifting hair
from neck and
running my finger
gently there. Across
the line of
clavicle.
Down curve of rib.
Following
concave of waist
coming to rest on
the hard of hip.
Revel, now
in the shiver that
rises
along your spine.
It means you are awake.

this body is not the enemy
your sex is not a scandal
your skin needs no censor
you are not here for denial
your pleasure is
what the universe
demands
it is the purpose
of your
creation
anything else
is
blasphemy
so tattoo want along your rib
name it religion and church
and the rite of communion
take the body and the blood
sprinkle it with holy water
let the salt steam rise
and listen
just listen, lover
always
our bodies tell us
where
to
begin.

Hold your capacity for melancholy
and name it strength.
Hold your righteous anger
and name it the pathway to peace.
Honor your translucent skin,
your bone-truth bruises.
Worship your geography
of bones and scars
that roadmap of veins,
the path to the center,
the pulse of spirit,
the gateway of want.
Light torch to
bonds built from lies,
let the flames build.
Ignite truth
and let it burn.
Merge ashes into melody,
knit moments into worlds,
howl visions into open skies.
Fold yourself into the endless rain
and call the wild things home.

This is an invitation.
Enter your life now.
Build a home inside your hollow.
Cast a spell into the ether.
Evoke your own divinity.
Turn the music up loud,
let it build.
Feel the reverb
settle deep in your bones,
until your spirit
pulsates.
Until the heat of it
permeates
your entire existence.
Listen, you starlight seeker.
Listen, you jackhammer goddess.
You've been holding on tightly
to things no longer yours.
Loosen your grip, lover,
ease open your palms.
Come out with your hands up.
This is not arrest.
This is the beginning.

AND YOU MUST NOT BE TAMED.

She lives transparent now.
Welcomes the feel
of air on bare skin.
Throws arms wide.
Holds out her heart
and says here,
take this.
All of it.
She figured early
that far too much energy
is invested in veiling
truth.
In hiding bodies.
In cloaking love.
She refuses
to cultivate shame.
She saves her effort for
vital things.

Let's get this clear right now. You do not have to say yes to grow. You do not have to say yes to be brave. You do not have to say yes to everything in order to move mountains or be wild or succulent or true.

NO CAN BE A PROFOUNDLY POWERFUL WORD.

FORGET WHAT THEY TOLD YOU.

You are the love child of a passionate affair between goddess and universe. You were born of a steamy forbidden heat and you were made for the cyclone of unadulterated wholeness. You are a daughter of delight. You are the unconstrained mother of all.

A fierce warrior. A wicked priestess. Your roots twist into this earth. Your spirit rises in glorious asana. You let loose with the howl of the wilderness you've held tight all these years.

YOU ARE WILD. UNTETHERED. GLORIOUSLY FREE.

YOU ARE NOT TOO MUCH.

You have never been too much. You will never be too much. The very idea is preposterous. Because you were born to be you. All of you. Not a tiny acceptable sliver. Not a watered-down version with colors dulled and edges softened. No. You were meant to be every last pulsing-bleeding-loving-crying-feeling bit.

ACKNOWLEDGEMENTS

My daughters, Julianna and Isabella. Thank you for being the greatest teachers I could ever have. For accepting the long hours at the keyboard, for loving me so deeply and fiercely, for cuddles in the marshmallow bed and for resolutely insisting on your truth with all of your beings, and for showing me how to do the same. I would not be the writer or the woman that I am without your love. You are my holiest gifts.

For Sam, for your steadfast and rock-solid dedication to our girls and for supporting my work in countless ways. I am eternally grateful.

To my family:
My parents, Jeff and Doreen. Thank you for raising me to question authority and always honor my roots, for filling our home with craziness and music and love, and for allowing me infinite space to grow and fumble and become. My brothers Andrew and Mark and especially my sister Lynn (thanks for loving me more).

To the ones who know me best, see me completely and love me always - my witches, my tribe, my five-pointed star, my inner circle. My eternal cheerleaders, my last minute babysitters, my chosen family, my roots and wings. Your names are too many to list here, but every last one of you is forever imprinted on my soul.

Most especially:
Leigh Steele, Marybeth Bonfiglio, Jessamyn Turgeson, Maisha Hairston, Winona Gray, Mani Schwartz, Carena Queskia, Jen Cody, Karen Bayless Feldman, Rachael Maddox, Chris Pruitt, Crowe Withane, Nikki Creason, Aimee Hansen, Dolly Mahtani, Krista Roscoe, Kimberley Hunter, Amy Birks, Jen Turrell.

My Wild Heart Writers. You took my questions and unleashed your stories. Together we created something larger and more magical than I ever could have dreamed, all with the power of your words and your love. You ARE writers, every last one, and my wild heart is yours forever and ever and always.

For everyone who worked to make this book a reality:

Stacy de la Rosa - the best book midwide a girl could dream of and deeply cherished friend. To long polos, endless text streams and every bit of love it took to bring this book into the world. Thank you. Thank you. A million times over, thank you.

My editors - Beth Riley, Shanna Atchley, Courtney Quinlan and Erica Wheadon. Thank god people like you exist, to save people like me from your own mistakes To me, you are all magical unicorns, and I am forever grateful. Don't ever go anywhere. I need you.

Jacob Nordy: you were not the first person to tell me I should write a book, but you were the first person to sit me down and show me how it could happen. Your belief in me changed everything. I cannot thank you enough for your mentorship, guidance and friendship.

Lidia Yuknavitch, Andrea Gibson, Brian Andreas. Each of you has created work in the world that opened me, inspired me, and forever changed me as a writer and as a human. My gratitude to your for the work you do in this world cannot wrap itself in mere words, but I send it out into the cosmos and trust you know exactly how much it matters that you do what you do. I'm blessed to call your friends, but I know I'll be fangirling until the end of time.

To the staff, baristas and people of Lux. A great many of the lines in this book were written inside your walls, soaking in the buzz of activity, and nursing endless almond milk lattes. Thank you for the free refills, the paleo cookies and the energy of inspiration.

In this life I have been loved in ways that have cracked me open, and broken me down that delivered me to hope, that made all things possible. All of those loves are present within the words of this book. For that I give thanks here, and in the spaces that live beyond the words.

For every person everywhere who ever read my words and found a small home for themselves inside of the lines I have written. Without you my writing would only ever be half alive. You are the other piece of the puzzle, the reflection in the mirror. Thank you for receiving my offering, and for holding it with such care.

For everyone who has taken time to write or email or comment to let me know that my words have made a difference. You may not know this, but for many years I have copied and pasted your words into a document that I keep carefully folded in a drawer by my bed. During many a 3am reckoning it is your words I have taken out to read and reread to remind me why I must continue to write into the center of it all and the everything. When you take the time to let an artist know their work matters, you become a part of their work, and you are forever a part of mine.

For everyone who writes and creates despite the risk and regardless of the cost, you are the courage in my veins and the reason I know I must keep on doing this. Do not stop ever creating. We all find our home inside of stories, please keep telling yours.

In Memory of Dana O'Dell. Forever Beautiful Real.

Jeanette LeBlanc spent most of her years working very hard to be a good girl. One day she woke up, and decided to writer her way out of her own life. Things haven't been the same since. A single mama to two ridiculously unruly children, Jeanette believes in the smooth honey burn of whiskey, the crashing of ocean waves, pencil skirts, vintage band tees and fringed boots, the kinship of the wild wolf, walking for miles in unfamiliar cities, the power of dark read lipstick and the necessity of putting out for the muse on the regular.

jeanetteleblanc.com